AF255748

Recognizing a year of blessings from your Savior

Heather R. Elizabeth Fowler

McKenzie Jotina Elizabeth Fowler

ISBN: 978-0-578-87275-9

From Heather and McKenzie,

We are so excited you have purchased this prayer journal. As a mother and daughter, we have talked about the Lord's presence in our lives for years. We love to call each other after we see the unmistakable presence of the Lord in our life. We call those times, "God Winks."

We have designed this prayer journal as a daily workbook to help you start to see just how close the Creator of the Universe is to your heart. You will see, as we have, that using this guide daily will help you see those places Jesus made Himself known to you throughout your day. After a few weeks of this practice, it can also help you be strong and courageous without fear (Deuteronomy 31:6), because you have seen the proof of His existence in your daily life. Through this journal, you can go back and see past examples of His amazing grace where He has made a difference in your life and the lives of those you love.

Let's face it, there is going to be trouble in this life (John 16:33), but when you can see the difference that the Lord's presence has made in your life, your doubt, fear, anxiety and discouragement will lessen.

We are excited for you to get started.

Blessings,
Heather and McKenzie Fowler

The Power of Prayer

As Christians we pray. Some of us pray only during church, others before every meal, some pray during a daily quiet time, and then others feel like they pray constantly. But here's a question that might stop and make you think: "Why do we pray?" Do we think we will change God's mind on a subject? Do we pray to point God to an event or situation that He doesn't know about? Of course, my first response is, "No! God knows everything, and His actions and decisions are perfect!" But then the question still looms, why do we pray? After digging deep and pondering the question, I came up with 4 major points:

1. **I pray to have a growing thriving relationship with Jesus.** My husband was a Christian from the age of seven. By the time I met him, he had been a believer for fourteen years. His faith was completely grounded. He knew who Jesus is and lived without doubt. I wanted that, and accepted Christ when I was twenty-three. The unshakable, no doubt, kind of faith wasn't mine from the moment of acceptance, but it is now. I know who Jesus is because I talk to Him constantly. I tell Him thank you, I ask for help with decisions, and I ask for help with family and friends' issues. In addition to that, I love just sitting with Him and listening.

2. **Prayer helps us see God's ability to change our circumstances.** I have a prayer wall in my house. Whenever someone asks for prayer, I put the prayer on a piece of paper and add their request

to the wall. When I walk down the hall, God always points out a person to pray for. When God says "Yes" to the prayer, it is moved to another, always growing, side of the wall. A few months ago, I was literally prostrate on the ground in prayer for a family member. I was distressed. Then the Holy Spirit lifted my head and showed me the wall plastered with answered prayer requests. It came to me like a bolt of lightning, "God has helped all those people, why am I doubting his help for one more?"

3. **Prayer reminds us who is in control.** The power of prayer is in the One who hears it. Our prayers will not change God's mind, they exemplify His power. God's plan is perfect, and He works everything for good for those who love Him and called according to His purpose (Romans 8:28). So, the question remains if we cannot change His mind, why do we pray? I have a prayer that I have prayed for my son since he was diagnosed with a disorder fourteen years ago. Every time I have prayed, I feel the answer has been the same, "Not yet." I would love for my son to be healed, but I look back at what God has accomplished through his disorder and I am grateful beyond words that my Lord and Savior is control.

4. **I pray for the honor and privilege of being a part of God's plan.** The most precious part of my life is being used by my Savior to further His plan on Earth. God commands us to pray. Philippians 4:6-7 says, "Do not be anxious about anything, but in every situation, by prayer and petition, with thanksgiving, present your requests to God. And the peace of God, which transcends all understanding, will guard your hearts and your minds in Christ Jesus."

When we pray, we are obeying our Heavenly Father. In return, He gives us peace and joy beyond understanding.

How to Use this Journal

This journal is designed to only take 5-10 minutes to complete each day. You will get something out of it whether you complete all sections each day or just have enough time to focus on one.

Date: It is important not to overlook this simple step. A date anchors the events of the day to the future you. It helps you look back on an event that happened and see how God was present even through the difficulty and helped you overcome it. We hope this will give you courage to confidently walk through any current event knowing that God has worked things for good in the past, why would He stop there? If it's not good, He's not finished.

People on My Heart: In this space, you will write one or two names of people God places on your heart. Not sure who He wants you to check on today? Be still and ask Him. Be sure to send a text to that person at some time during the day. Tell them that God placed them on your heart. Ask them if there is any way you can pray for them; and then do so.

Gratitude: Gratitude is one of the most powerful tools our Lord gives us. I try to live a life with gratitude always on my heart, but when I am discouraged, worried, or feeling weak, I especially rely on this mindset. In the space provided, write down a few of the things that you are thankful for that day. Please don't think they need to be eloquent, fancy thoughts. This is a space to allow your soul to talk. Write down the first things that come to mind.

God Winks: God winks are a concept that our family has thought, talked, and acted upon for years. When writing this prayer journal, we decided early on that God winks had to play a part, but as for a definition, that had to be worked on. We knew what it meant, but describing it was tricky. This is what we came up with: A God wink is a moment in your day where God makes Himself known. We can see God while hiking in His beautiful creation. We can see Him through moments of kindness by others. We can also see God through divine providence. Divine providence is where God works events through natural means to have a certain outcome transpire. Divine providence happens all around us, but it often takes us intentionally looking for it, for us to see it.

Prayer Requests: In this prayer request space, we encourage you to not only write your own prayer requests but also write down the requests of others. It could be something that someone has already asked for your prayer on or you could reach out to the names you wrote above in the "On My Heart" section. Write the requests down, and actively pray for them. Regularly flip back through the pages and ask God to help you focus on the people you need to lift up to Him. Then the fun part: check up on past prayers and check off the ones that were answered "Yes". We believe that God answers every prayer. Sometimes the answer is "Yes", sometimes "No", and sometimes "Not yet". By keeping track of prayer requests, you'll be able to see how God is present and active in your life and the lives of those around you. We might not get the answers we want at the speed we want them, but He is always listening and always answering our prayers. He is a present and active God.

Date __________________________

People on My Heart:

____
____
____

Gratitude

God Winks:

Prayer Requests:

* __________________________ ◊

* __________________________ ◊

* __________________________ ◊

Date ________________________

People on My Heart:

____
____
____

Gratitude

God Winks:

Prayer Requests:

* ________________________ ◊
* ________________________ ◊
* ________________________ ◊

Date ______________________________

People on My Heart:

____

____

____

Gratitude

God Winks:

Prayer Requests:

* ____________________ ◇

* ____________________ ◇

* ____________________ ◇

Date __________________________

People on My Heart:

____

____

____

Gratitude

God Winks:

Prayer Requests:

* __________________________ ◊

* __________________________ ◊

* __________________________ ◊

Date _______________________________

People on My Heart:

____

____

____

Gratitude

God Winks:

Prayer Requests:

* _______________________________

* _______________________________

* _______________________________

Date _______________________________

People on My Heart:

____

____

____

Gratitude

God Winks:

Prayer Requests:

* _______________________________ ◊

* _______________________________ ◊

* _______________________________ ◊

Date ______________________________

People on My Heart:

____
____
____

Gratitude

God Winks:

Prayer Requests:

* ______________________
* ______________________
* ______________________

Date ___________________________________

People on My Heart:

____

____

____

Gratitude

God Winks:

Prayer Requests:

* ___________________________________ ◊

* ___________________________________ ◊

* ___________________________________ ◊

Date _______________________________

People on My Heart:

____

____

____

Gratitude

God Winks:

Prayer Requests:

* _______________________________

* _______________________________

* _______________________________

Date _______________________________

People on My Heart:

____
____
____

Gratitude

God Winks:

Prayer Requests:

* _______________
* _______________
* _______________

Date ________________________________

People on My Heart:

____

____

____

Gratitude

God Winks:

Prayer Requests:

* ________________________________

* ________________________________

* ________________________________

Date _______________________________

People on My Heart:

____
____
____

Gratitude

God Winks:

Prayer Requests:

Date _______________________

People on My Heart:
____
____
____

Gratitude

God Winks:

Prayer Requests:

* _______________________
* _______________________
* _______________________

Date ___________________________

People on My Heart:

____
____
____

Gratitude

God Winks:

Prayer Requests:

* ___________________________

* ___________________________

* ___________________________

Date ___________________________

People on My Heart:

____

____

____

Gratitude

God Winks:

Prayer Requests:

* ___________________________ ◇

* ___________________________ ◇

* ___________________________ ◇

Date _______________________

People on My Heart:

____
____
____

Gratitude

God Winks:

Prayer Requests:

* _______________________
* _______________________
* _______________________

Date ______________________________

People on My Heart:

____
____
____

Gratitude

God Winks:

Prayer Requests:

* ______________________________
____

* ______________________________
____

* ______________________________
____

Date ______________________________

People on My Heart:

____
____
____

Gratitude

God Winks:

Prayer Requests:

* ______________________________
____

* ______________________________
____

* ______________________________
____

Date ___________________________

People on My Heart:

____

____

____

Gratitude

God Winks:

Prayer Requests:

* ___________________________

* ___________________________

* ___________________________

Date ___________________________

People on My Heart:

____

____

____

Gratitude

God Winks:

Prayer Requests:

* ___________________

* ___________________

* ___________________

Date ________________________

People on My Heart:

____

____

____

Gratitude

God Winks:

Prayer Requests:

* ___________________ ◇

* ___________________ ◇

* ___________________ ◇

Date _______________________________

People on My Heart:

Gratitude

God Winks:

Prayer Requests:

*
*
*

Date __________________________________

People on My Heart:

____

____

____

Gratitude

God Winks:

Prayer Requests:

* __________________________________ ◊

* __________________________________ ◊

* __________________________________ ◊

Date _______________________________

People on My Heart:

____

____

____

Gratitude

God Winks:

Prayer Requests:

* _______________________________ ◇

* _______________________________ ◇

* _______________________________ ◇

Date __________________________

People on My Heart:

____

____

____

Gratitude

God Winks:

Prayer Requests:

* __________________________ ◊

* __________________________ ◊

* __________________________ ◊

Date ______________________________

People on My Heart:

____

____

____

Gratitude

God Winks:

Prayer Requests:

* ______________________

* ______________________

* ______________________

Date _______________________________

People on My Heart:

Gratitude

God Winks:

Prayer Requests:

* ◇
* ◇
* ◇

Date ________________________________

People on My Heart:

Gratitude

God Winks:

Prayer Requests:

* ________________________________

* ________________________________

* ________________________________

Date ___________________________

People on My Heart:

____

____

____

Gratitude

God Winks:

Prayer Requests:

* ___________________________ ◊

* ___________________________ ◊

* ___________________________ ◊

Date _______________________________

People on My Heart:

____
____
____

Gratitude

God Winks:

Prayer Requests:

* _______________________________ ◊
* _______________________________ ◊
* _______________________________ ◊

Date ______________________________

People on My Heart:

____

____

____

Gratitude

God Winks:

Prayer Requests:

* ____________________

* ____________________

* ____________________

Date _______________________________

People on My Heart:

____

____

____

Gratitude

God Winks:

Prayer Requests:

* _______________________________________ ◊

* _______________________________________ ◊

* _______________________________________ ◊

Date ___________________________

People on My Heart:

____

____

____

Gratitude

God Winks:

Prayer Requests:

* ___________________________________

* ___________________________________

* ___________________________________

Date ________________________________

People on My Heart:

____

____

____

Gratitude

God Winks:

Prayer Requests:

* _______________________

* _______________________

* _______________________

Date _______________________

People on My Heart:

____

____

____

Gratitude

God Winks:

Prayer Requests:

* _______________________

* _______________________

* _______________________

Date ________________________

People on My Heart:

Gratitude

God Winks:

Prayer Requests:

*
*
*

Date ___________________________

People on My Heart:

____
____
____

Gratitude

God Winks:

Prayer Requests:

* ___________________________
* ___________________________
* ___________________________

Date _______________________________

People on My Heart:

____

____

____

Gratitude

God Winks:

Prayer Requests:

* _______________________

* _______________________

* _______________________

Date _______________________________

People on My Heart:

Gratitude

God Winks:

Prayer Requests:

Date ________________________________

People on My Heart:

____

____

____

Gratitude

God Winks:

Prayer Requests:

* ________________________________ ◊

* ________________________________ ◊

* ________________________________ ◊

Date _______________________________

People on My Heart:

____
____
____

Gratitude

God Winks:

Prayer Requests:

* _______________________________ ◊
____

* _______________________________ ◊
____

* _______________________________ ◊
____

Date _______________________________

People on My Heart:

____

____

____

Gratitude

God Winks:

Prayer Requests:

* ___________________________ ◇

* ___________________________ ◇

* ___________________________ ◇

Date ___________________________

People on My Heart:

____
____
____

Gratitude

God Winks:

Prayer Requests:

* ___________________________ ◊
* ___________________________ ◊
* ___________________________ ◊

Date ___________________________

People on My Heart:

____

____

____

Gratitude

God Winks:

Prayer Requests:

* ___________________________ ◇

* ___________________________ ◇

* ___________________________ ◇

Date ________________________________

People on My Heart:

____

____

____

Gratitude

God Winks:

Prayer Requests:

* ________________________________

* ________________________________

* ________________________________

Date _______________________________

People on My Heart:

____

____

____

Gratitude

God Winks:

Prayer Requests:

* _______________________

* _______________________

* _______________________

Date ___________________________

People on My Heart:

____

____

____

Gratitude

God Winks:

Prayer Requests:

* ___________________

* ___________________

* ___________________

Date _______________________________

People on My Heart:

____

____

____

Gratitude

God Winks:

Prayer Requests:

* _______________________________

* _______________________________

* _______________________________

Date ___________________________

People on My Heart:

____
____
____

Gratitude

God Winks:

Prayer Requests:

* ___________________
* ___________________
* ___________________

Date ________________________________

People on My Heart:

Gratitude

God Winks:

Prayer Requests:

Date _______________________________

People on My Heart:

____
____
____

Gratitude

God Winks:

Prayer Requests:

* _______________________________ ◊
* _______________________________ ◊
* _______________________________ ◊

Date ______________________________

People on My Heart:

____

____

____

Gratitude

God Winks:

Prayer Requests:

* ___________________________________ ◇

* ___________________________________ ◇

* ___________________________________ ◇

Date _______________________________

People on My Heart:

____

____

____

Gratitude

God Winks:

Prayer Requests:

* _______________________________

* _______________________________

* _______________________________

Date ______________________________

People on My Heart:

____
____
____

Gratitude

God Winks:

Prayer Requests:

* ______________________________ ◊
* ______________________________ ◊
* ______________________________ ◊

Date ___________________________

People on My Heart:

____

____

____

Gratitude

God Winks:

Prayer Requests:

* ___________________________

* ___________________________

* ___________________________

Date _______________________

People on My Heart:

____
____
____

Gratitude

God Winks:

Prayer Requests:

* _______________________
____

* _______________________
____

* _______________________
____

Date _______________________________

People on My Heart:

____

____

____

Gratitude

God Winks:

Prayer Requests:

* _______________________________ ◊

* _______________________________ ◊

* _______________________________ ◊

Date ___________________________

People on My Heart:

____
____
____

Gratitude

God Winks:

Prayer Requests:

* ___________________________ ◇
* ___________________________ ◇
* ___________________________ ◇

Date _______________________

People on My Heart:

____

____

____

Gratitude

God Winks:

Prayer Requests:

* ______________________◇

* ______________________◇

* ______________________◇

Date ________________________________

People on My Heart:

____

____

____

Gratitude

God Winks:

Prayer Requests:

* ________________________________ ◊

* ________________________________ ◊

* ________________________________ ◊

Date ________________________

People on My Heart:

____
____
____

Gratitude

God Winks:

Prayer Requests:

* ________________________
____

* ________________________
____

* ________________________
____

Date _______________________________

People on My Heart:

Gratitude

God Winks:

Prayer Requests:

*

*

*

Date ___________________________

People on My Heart:

____

____

____

Gratitude

God Winks:

Prayer Requests:

* ___________________________

* ___________________________

* ___________________________

Date _______________________________

People on My Heart:

____
____
____

Gratitude

God Winks:

Prayer Requests:

* _______________________ ◇
* _______________________ ◇
* _______________________ ◇

Date ___________________________

People on My Heart:

____

____

____

Gratitude

God Winks:

Prayer Requests:

* _______________________

* _______________________

* _______________________

Date ______________________________

People on My Heart:

____
____
____

Gratitude

God Winks:

Prayer Requests:

* ______________________________ ◊
* ______________________________ ◊
* ______________________________ ◊

Date _______________________________

People on My Heart:

Gratitude

God Winks:

Prayer Requests:

* _______________________________
* _______________________________
* _______________________________

Date _______________________________

People on My Heart:

Gratitude

God Winks:

Prayer Requests:

Date ___________________________

People on My Heart:

____
____
____

Gratitude

God Winks:

Prayer Requests:

* _______________________ ◊
* _______________________ ◊
* _______________________ ◊

Date ______________________________

People on My Heart:

____

____

____

Gratitude

God Winks:

Prayer Requests:

* ______________________________ ◊

* ______________________________ ◊

* ______________________________ ◊

Date _______________________________

People on My Heart:

____

____

____

Gratitude

God Winks:

Prayer Requests:

* _______________________________ ◊

* _______________________________ ◊

* _______________________________ ◊

Date ___________________________

People on My Heart:
____
____
____

Gratitude

God Winks:

Prayer Requests:

* _______________________________ ◊
____

* _______________________________ ◊
____

* _______________________________ ◊
____

Date ___________________________

People on My Heart:

____
____
____

Gratitude

God Winks:

Prayer Requests:

* ___________________________
* ___________________________
* ___________________________

Date _______________________________

People on My Heart:

____

____

____

Gratitude

God Winks:

Prayer Requests:

* _______________________________

* _______________________________

* _______________________________

Date ________________________________

People on My Heart:

____

____

____

Gratitude

God Winks:

Prayer Requests:

* ________________________

* ________________________

* ________________________

Date ___________________________

People on My Heart:

____

____

____

Gratitude

God Winks:

Prayer Requests:

* ___________________________

* ___________________________

* ___________________________

Date ________________________________

People on My Heart:

Gratitude

God Winks:

Prayer Requests:

*

*

*

Date ___________________________

People on My Heart:

____

____

____

Gratitude

God Winks:

Prayer Requests:

* ______________________

* ______________________

* ______________________

Date _______________________________

People on My Heart:

____
____
____

Gratitude

God Winks:

Prayer Requests:

* ___________________________
* ___________________________
* ___________________________

Date ___________________________

People on My Heart:

____

____

____

Gratitude

God Winks:

Prayer Requests:

* ___________________________ ◊

* ___________________________ ◊

* ___________________________ ◊

Date _______________________

People on My Heart:

Gratitude

God Winks:

Prayer Requests:

*
*
*

Date _______________________________

People on My Heart:

____

____

____

Gratitude

God Winks:

Prayer Requests:

* _______________________ ◊

* _______________________ ◊

* _______________________ ◊

Date _______________________________

People on My Heart:

____

____

____

Gratitude

God Winks:

Prayer Requests:

* ____________________

* ____________________

* ____________________

Date _______________________________

People on My Heart:
____
____
____

Gratitude

God Winks:

Prayer Requests:

* _______________________________
* _______________________________
* _______________________________

Date ______________________________

People on My Heart:

Gratitude

God Winks:

Prayer Requests:

*
*
*

Date ___________________________

People on My Heart:

____

____

____

Gratitude

God Winks:

Prayer Requests:

* ___________________________

* ___________________________

* ___________________________

Date __________________________

People on My Heart:

Gratitude

God Winks:

Prayer Requests:

Date _______________________________

People on My Heart:

Gratitude

God Winks:

Prayer Requests:

*
*
*

Date ___________________________

People on My Heart:

____
____
____

Gratitude

God Winks:

Prayer Requests:

* ___________________________
* ___________________________
* ___________________________

Date ___________________________

People on My Heart:

____
____
____

Gratitude

God Winks:

Prayer Requests:

* ___________________________ ◊
* ___________________________ ◊
* ___________________________ ◊

Date _______________________________

People on My Heart:

____
____
____

Gratitude

God Winks:

Prayer Requests:

* _______________________________
* _______________________________
* _______________________________

Date _______________________________

People on My Heart:

Gratitude

God Winks:

Prayer Requests:

Date ___________________________

People on My Heart:

____
____
____

Gratitude

God Winks:

Prayer Requests:

* _______________________________________ ◊
* _______________________________________ ◊
* _______________________________________ ◊

Date ___________________________

People on My Heart:

____
____
____

Gratitude

God Winks:

Prayer Requests:

* ___________________________ ◇

* ___________________________ ◇

* ___________________________ ◇

Date _______________________________

People on My Heart:

____

____

____

Gratitude

God Winks:

Prayer Requests:

*_______________________

*_______________________

*_______________________

Date ______________________________

People on My Heart:

____

____

____

Gratitude

God Winks:

Prayer Requests:

* ______________________________ ◊

* ______________________________ ◊

* ______________________________ ◊

Date ___________________________

People on My Heart:

____
____
____

Gratitude

God Winks:

Prayer Requests:

* ___________________________
____

* ___________________________
____

* ___________________________
____

Date ___________________________

People on My Heart:

____
____
____

Gratitude

God Winks:

Prayer Requests:

* ___________________________
____

* ___________________________
____

* ___________________________
____

Date _______________________________

People on My Heart:

____

____

____

Gratitude

God Winks:

Prayer Requests:

* _______________________________ ◊

* _______________________________ ◊

* _______________________________ ◊

Date _______________________________

People on My Heart:

____
____
____

Gratitude

God Winks:

Prayer Requests:

* _______________________________ ◇
* _______________________________ ◇
* _______________________________ ◇

Date ________________________________

People on My Heart:

____

____

____

Gratitude

God Winks:

Prayer Requests:

* ________________________________ ◊

* ________________________________ ◊

* ________________________________ ◊

Date ______________________________

People on My Heart:

____
____
____

Gratitude

God Winks:

Prayer Requests:

* ______________________ ◊
* ______________________ ◊
* ______________________ ◊

Date ___________________________

People on My Heart:

____

____

____

Gratitude

God Winks:

Prayer Requests:

* ___________________________

* ___________________________

* ___________________________

Date ___________________________

People on My Heart:

____
____
____

Gratitude

God Winks:

Prayer Requests:

* ___________________________
____

* ___________________________
____

* ___________________________
____

Date ___________________________

People on My Heart:

____
____
____

Gratitude

God Winks:

Prayer Requests:

* _______________________________ ◊
* _______________________________ ◊
* _______________________________ ◊

Date ________________________________

People on My Heart:

____

____

____

Gratitude

God Winks:

Prayer Requests:

* ________________________ ◊

* ________________________ ◊

* ________________________ ◊

Date ___________________________

People on My Heart:

____

____

____

Gratitude

God Winks:

Prayer Requests:

* ___________________________

* ___________________________

* ___________________________

Date ___________________________

People on My Heart:

____
____
____

Gratitude

God Winks:

Prayer Requests:

* ___________________________ ◇
* ___________________________ ◇
* ___________________________ ◇

Date ______________________________

People on My Heart:

____

____

____

Gratitude

God Winks:

Prayer Requests:

* ______________________________ ◇

* ______________________________ ◇

* ______________________________ ◇

Date _______________________________

People on My Heart:

____
____
____

Gratitude

God Winks:

Prayer Requests:

* _______________________________ ◊
* _______________________________ ◊
* _______________________________ ◊

Date _______________________________

People on My Heart:

____

____

____

Gratitude

God Winks:

Prayer Requests:

* _______________________________ ◊

* _______________________________ ◊

* _______________________________ ◊

Date _______________________

People on My Heart:

____
____
____

Gratitude

God Winks:

Prayer Requests:

* _______________________ ◇
* _______________________ ◇
* _______________________ ◇

Date _______________________

People on My Heart:

____
____
____

Gratitude

God Winks:

Prayer Requests:

* ________________________
* ________________________
* ________________________

Date _______________________

People on My Heart:

____
____
____

Gratitude

God Winks:

Prayer Requests:

* _______________________ ◊
____

* _______________________ ◊
____

* _______________________ ◊
____

Date _______________________

People on My Heart:

____

____

____

Gratitude

God Winks:

Prayer Requests:

* _______________________

* _______________________

* _______________________

Date ___________________________

People on My Heart:

____

____

____

Gratitude

God Winks:

Prayer Requests:

* ___________________________ ◊

* ___________________________ ◊

* ___________________________ ◊

Date _______________________________

People on My Heart:

____
____
____

Gratitude

God Winks:

Prayer Requests:

* _______________________
* _______________________
* _______________________

Date ___________________________________

People on My Heart:

____

____

____

Gratitude

God Winks:

Prayer Requests:

* ___________________________________ ◇

* ___________________________________ ◇

* ___________________________________ ◇

Date ___________________________

People on My Heart:

____
____
____

Gratitude

God Winks:

Prayer Requests:

* ___________________________ ◇
* ___________________________ ◇
* ___________________________ ◇

Date ___________________________________

People on My Heart:

____

____

____

Gratitude

God Winks:

Prayer Requests:

* ___________________________________ ◊

* ___________________________________ ◊

* ___________________________________ ◊

Date ___________________________

People on My Heart:

Gratitude

God Winks:

Prayer Requests:

*
*
*

Date ___________________________

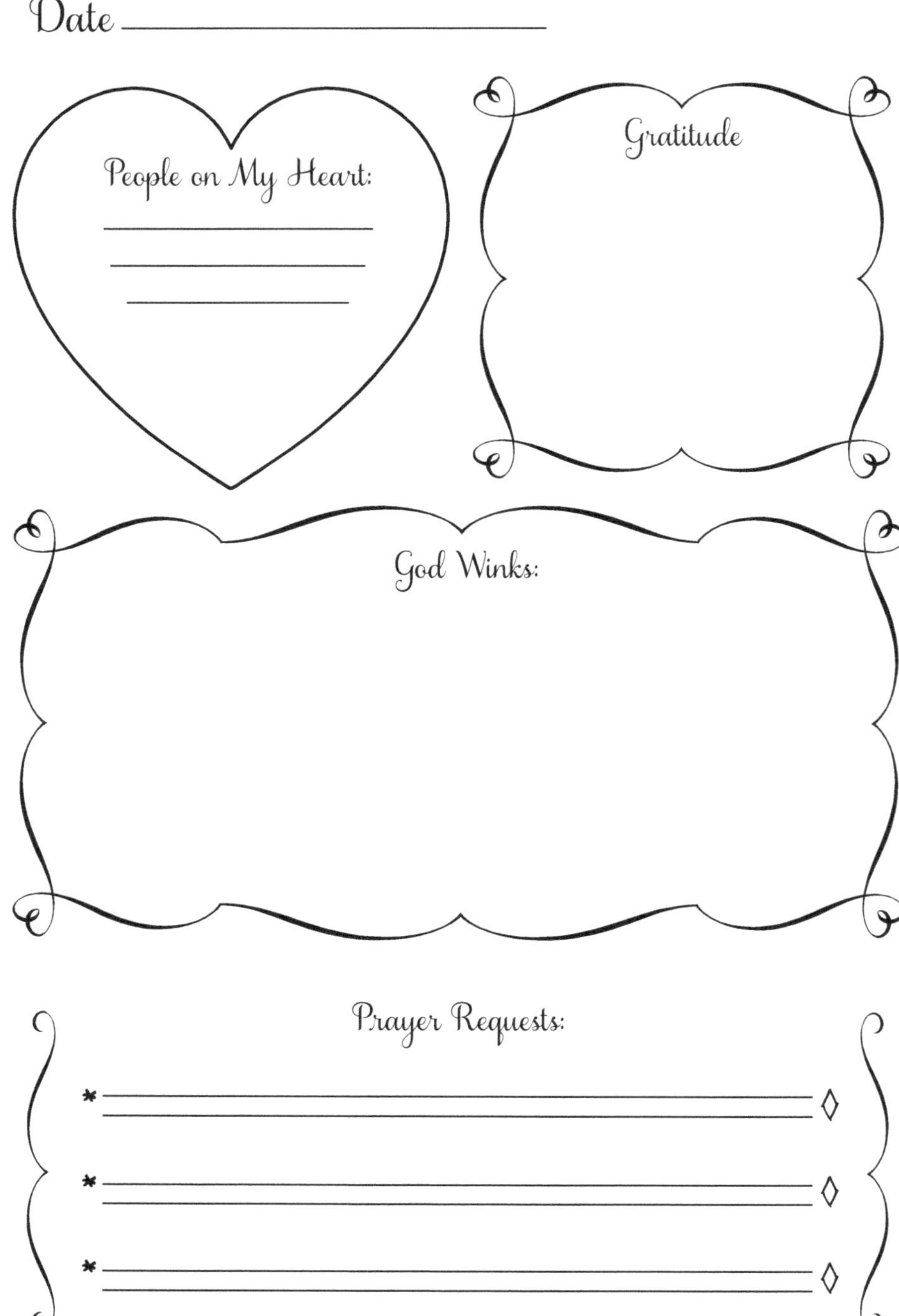

Date ______________________________

People on My Heart:

____
____
____

Gratitude

God Winks:

Prayer Requests:

* ______________________________ ◊
____

* ______________________________ ◊
____

* ______________________________ ◊
____

Date _______________________

People on My Heart:

____
____
____

Gratitude

God Winks:

Prayer Requests:

* _______________________ ◊
* _______________________ ◊
* _______________________ ◊

Date ________________________________

People on My Heart:

____

____

____

Gratitude

God Winks:

Prayer Requests:

* ________________________________ ◊

* ________________________________ ◊

* ________________________________ ◊

Date ________________________________

People on My Heart:

____
____
____

Gratitude

God Winks:

Prayer Requests:

* ________________________ ◊
* ________________________ ◊
* ________________________ ◊

Date _______________________________

People on My Heart:

Gratitude

God Winks:

Prayer Requests:

*
*
*

Date ______________________________

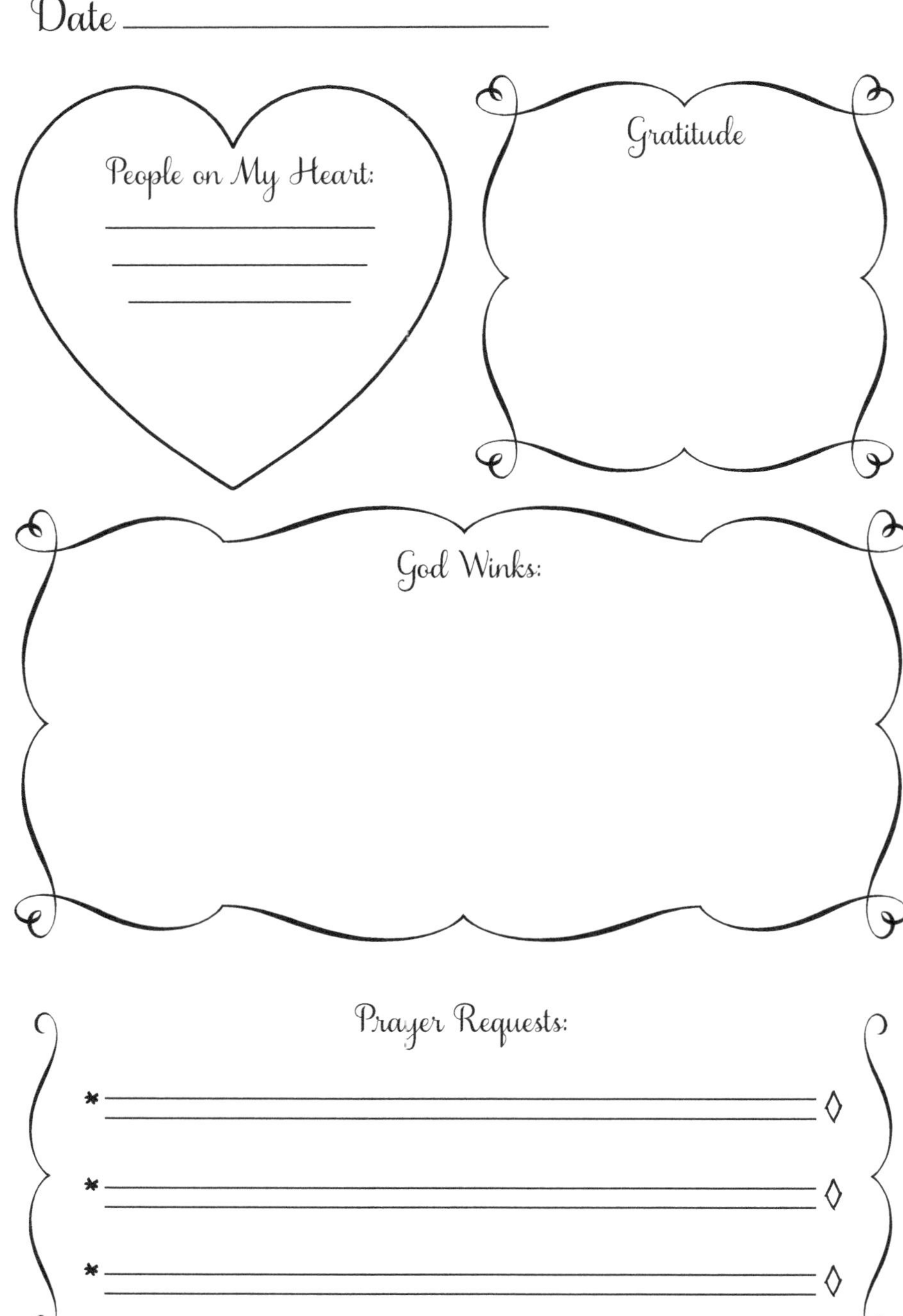

Date _______________________________

People on My Heart:

____

____

____

Gratitude

God Winks:

Prayer Requests:

* _______________________________________ ◊

* _______________________________________ ◊

* _______________________________________ ◊

Date ___________________________

People on My Heart:

____

____

____

Gratitude

God Winks:

Prayer Requests:

* ___________________________ ◊

* ___________________________ ◊

* ___________________________ ◊

Date _______________________________

People on My Heart:

Gratitude

God Winks:

Prayer Requests:

* _______________________________
* _______________________________
* _______________________________

Date ___________________________

People on My Heart:

____

____

____

Gratitude

God Winks:

Prayer Requests:

* ___________________________ ◊

* ___________________________ ◊

* ___________________________ ◊

Date _______________________________

People on My Heart:

____

____

____

Gratitude

God Winks:

Prayer Requests:

* _______________________________ ◇

* _______________________________ ◇

* _______________________________ ◇

Date ________________________________

People on My Heart:

Gratitude

God Winks:

Prayer Requests:

Date _______________________________

People on My Heart:

____

____

____

Gratitude

God Winks:

Prayer Requests:

* _______________________________ ◊

* _______________________________ ◊

* _______________________________ ◊

Date _______________________________

People on My Heart:

____

____

____

Gratitude

God Winks:

Prayer Requests:

* _______________________ ◊

* _______________________ ◊

* _______________________ ◊

Date ___________________________

People on My Heart:

____

____

____

Gratitude

God Winks:

Prayer Requests:

* ___________________________

* ___________________________

* ___________________________

Date _______________________

People on My Heart:

____
____
____

Gratitude

God Winks:

Prayer Requests:

* _______________________ ◇
____

* _______________________ ◇
____

* _______________________ ◇
____

Date ______________________________

People on My Heart:

Gratitude

God Winks:

Prayer Requests:

* ______________________________

* ______________________________

* ______________________________

Date ________________________________

People on My Heart:

____

____

____

Gratitude

God Winks:

Prayer Requests:

* ____________________

* ____________________

* ____________________

Date ______________________________

People on My Heart:

____

____

____

Gratitude

God Winks:

Prayer Requests:

* ______________________________ ◊

* ______________________________ ◊

* ______________________________ ◊

Date ______________________________

People on My Heart:

____

____

____

Gratitude

God Winks:

Prayer Requests:

* ______________________________

* ______________________________

* ______________________________

Date ________________________________

People on My Heart:

____

____

____

Gratitude

God Winks:

Prayer Requests:

* ________________________________

* ________________________________

* ________________________________

Date ___________________________

People on My Heart:

____

____

____

Gratitude

God Winks:

Prayer Requests:

* ___________________________

* ___________________________

* ___________________________

Date ________________________

People on My Heart:

____

____

____

Gratitude

God Winks:

Prayer Requests:

* ________________________

* ________________________

* ________________________

Date ________________________________

People on My Heart:

____

____

____

Gratitude

God Winks:

Prayer Requests:

* ____________________ ◇

* ____________________ ◇

* ____________________ ◇

Date ________________________

People on My Heart:

____

____

____

Gratitude

God Winks:

Prayer Requests:

* ________________________ ◊

* ________________________ ◊

* ________________________ ◊

Date ______________________________

People on My Heart:

____
____
____

Gratitude

God Winks:

Prayer Requests:

* ______________________________ ◇
* ______________________________ ◇
* ______________________________ ◇

Date ________________________________

People on My Heart:

____

____

____

Gratitude

God Winks:

Prayer Requests:

* ___________________________ ◊

* ___________________________ ◊

* ___________________________ ◊

Date ___________________________

People on My Heart:

____

____

____

Gratitude

God Winks:

Prayer Requests:

* _______________________ ◊

* _______________________ ◊

* _______________________ ◊

Date _______________________________

People on My Heart:

____
____
____

Gratitude

God Winks:

Prayer Requests:

* _______________________________
* _______________________________
* _______________________________

Date ___________________________

People on My Heart:

____
____
____

Gratitude

God Winks:

Prayer Requests:

* ___________________________
* ___________________________
* ___________________________

Date ___________________________

People on My Heart:

____

____

____

Gratitude

God Winks:

Prayer Requests:

*___________________________ ◇

*___________________________ ◇

*___________________________ ◇

Date ___________________________

People on My Heart:

____

____

____

Gratitude

God Winks:

Prayer Requests:

* ___________________________

* ___________________________

* ___________________________

Date ______________________________

People on My Heart:

____
____
____

Gratitude

God Winks:

Prayer Requests:

* ______________________________ ◊
* ______________________________ ◊
* ______________________________ ◊

Date ___________________________________

People on My Heart:

____

____

____

Gratitude

God Winks:

Prayer Requests:

* ___________________________________ ◊
____

* ___________________________________ ◊
____

* ___________________________________ ◊
____

Date _______________________________

People on My Heart:

Gratitude

God Winks:

Prayer Requests:

*

*

*

Date _______________________________

People on My Heart:
____
____
____

Gratitude

God Winks:

Prayer Requests:

* _______________________
* _______________________
* _______________________

Date _______________________________

People on My Heart:

____

____

____

Gratitude

God Winks:

Prayer Requests:

* _______________________________ ◊

* _______________________________ ◊

* _______________________________ ◊

Date _______________________________

People on My Heart:

____

____

____

Gratitude

God Winks:

Prayer Requests:

* _______________________________

* _______________________________

* _______________________________

Date _______________________________

People on My Heart:

____

____

____

Gratitude

God Winks:

Prayer Requests:

* _______________________

* _______________________

* _______________________

Date ______________________________

People on My Heart:

____
____
____

Gratitude

God Winks:

Prayer Requests:

* ______________________________ ◊

* ______________________________ ◊

* ______________________________ ◊

Date ___________________________

People on My Heart:

____

____

____

Gratitude

God Winks:

Prayer Requests:

* ___________________________

* ___________________________

* ___________________________

Date _______________________________

People on My Heart:

____

____

____

Gratitude

God Winks:

Prayer Requests:

* _______________________________

* _______________________________

* _______________________________

Date ______________________________

People on My Heart:

____

____

____

Gratitude

God Winks:

Prayer Requests:

* ___________________________________

* ___________________________________

* ___________________________________

Date _______________________

People on My Heart:

____
____
____

Gratitude

God Winks:

Prayer Requests:

* _______________________ ◊
____

* _______________________ ◊
____

* _______________________ ◊
____

Date _______________________________

People on My Heart:

Gratitude

God Winks:

Prayer Requests:

*
*
*

Date ___________________________

People on My Heart:

____

____

____

Gratitude

God Winks:

Prayer Requests:

* ___________________________

* ___________________________

* ___________________________

Date ______________________________

People on My Heart:

____
____
____

Gratitude

God Winks:

Prayer Requests:

* ______________________________
____

* ______________________________
____

* ______________________________
____

Date ___________________________

People on My Heart:

____

____

____

Gratitude

God Winks:

Prayer Requests:

* ___________________________ ◊

* ___________________________ ◊

* ___________________________ ◊

Date ___________________________

People on My Heart:

____

____

____

Gratitude

God Winks:

Prayer Requests:

* ___________________________ ◊

* ___________________________ ◊

* ___________________________ ◊

Date ______________________________

People on My Heart:

____
____
____

Gratitude

God Winks:

Prayer Requests:

* ______________________________
* ______________________________
* ______________________________

Date ______________________________

People on My Heart:

____

____

____

Gratitude

God Winks:

Prayer Requests:

* _______________________

* _______________________

* _______________________

Date _______________________________

People on My Heart:

____

____

____

Gratitude

God Winks:

Prayer Requests:

* _______________________________ ◇

* _______________________________ ◇

* _______________________________ ◇

Date _______________________

People on My Heart:

Gratitude

God Winks:

Prayer Requests:

*
*
*

Date ___________________________

People on My Heart:

____

____

____

Gratitude

God Winks:

Prayer Requests:

* ___________________________ ◊

* ___________________________ ◊

* ___________________________ ◊

Date ______________________________

People on My Heart:

____
____
____

Gratitude

God Winks:

Prayer Requests:

* ______________________________ ◊
* ______________________________ ◊
* ______________________________ ◊

Date ________________________________

People on My Heart:

____

____

____

Gratitude

God Winks:

Prayer Requests:

* ____________________________________

* ____________________________________

* ____________________________________

Date _______________________

People on My Heart:

____
____
____

Gratitude

God Winks:

Prayer Requests:

* _______________________
* _______________________
* _______________________

Date _______________________

People on My Heart:

____
____
____

Gratitude

God Winks:

Prayer Requests:

* _______________________
____

* _______________________
____

* _______________________
____

Date ___________________________

People on My Heart:

____

____

____

Gratitude

God Winks:

Prayer Requests:

* ___________________________

* ___________________________

* ___________________________

Date ___________________________________

People on My Heart:

____

____

____

Gratitude

God Winks:

Prayer Requests:

* _______________________

* _______________________

* _______________________

Date _______________________________

People on My Heart:

____

____

____

Gratitude

God Winks:

Prayer Requests:

* _______________________ ◇

* _______________________ ◇

* _______________________ ◇

Date _______________________________

People on My Heart:

Gratitude

God Winks:

Prayer Requests:

* _______________________________

* _______________________________

* _______________________________

Date _______________________

People on My Heart:

____
____
____

Gratitude

God Winks:

Prayer Requests:

* _______________________ ◊
* _______________________ ◊
* _______________________ ◊

Date ___________________________

People on My Heart:

Gratitude

God Winks:

Prayer Requests:

*
*
*

Date _______________________________

People on My Heart:

Gratitude

God Winks:

Prayer Requests:

* _______________________________
* _______________________________
* _______________________________

Date ___________________________

People on My Heart:

____
____
____

Gratitude

God Winks:

Prayer Requests:

* ___________________________

* ___________________________

* ___________________________

Date ________________________________

People on My Heart:

Gratitude

God Winks:

Prayer Requests:

* ________________________________ ◊

* ________________________________ ◊

* ________________________________ ◊

Date ___________________________

People on My Heart:

____

____

____

Gratitude

God Winks:

Prayer Requests:

* ______________________

* ______________________

* ______________________

Date ________________________________

People on My Heart:

____

____

____

Gratitude

God Winks:

Prayer Requests:

* _____________________

* _____________________

* _____________________

Date _______________________________

People on My Heart:

____

____

____

Gratitude

God Winks:

Prayer Requests:

* _______________________________ ◊

* _______________________________ ◊

* _______________________________ ◊

Date ______________________________

People on My Heart:

____
____
____

Gratitude

God Winks:

Prayer Requests:

* ___________________________________
* ___________________________________
* ___________________________________

Date ________________________________

People on My Heart:

____

____

____

Gratitude

God Winks:

Prayer Requests:

* ________________________ ◇

* ________________________ ◇

* ________________________ ◇

Date ______________________________

People on My Heart:

____

____

____

Gratitude

God Winks:

Prayer Requests:

* ______________________________ ◊

* ______________________________ ◊

* ______________________________ ◊

Date ______________________________

People on My Heart:

____
____
____

Gratitude

God Winks:

Prayer Requests:

* ______________________________
____

* ______________________________
____

* ______________________________
____

Date _______________________________

People on My Heart:

____

____

____

Gratitude

God Winks:

Prayer Requests:

* _______________________ ◊

* _______________________ ◊

* _______________________ ◊

Date _______________________

People on My Heart:

____

____

____

Gratitude

God Winks:

Prayer Requests:

* __________________________

* __________________________

* __________________________

Date ________________________________

People on My Heart:

____

____

____

Gratitude

God Winks:

Prayer Requests:

* ________________________________

* ________________________________

* ________________________________

Date ______________________________

People on My Heart:

____

____

____

Gratitude

God Winks:

Prayer Requests:

* ______________________________ ◇

* ______________________________ ◇

* ______________________________ ◇

Date ___________________________

People on My Heart:

____

____

____

Gratitude

God Winks:

Prayer Requests:

* ___________________________ ◊

* ___________________________ ◊

* ___________________________ ◊

Date ______________________________

People on My Heart:

____

____

____

Gratitude

God Winks:

Prayer Requests:

* ______________________________

* ______________________________

* ______________________________

Date ________________________

People on My Heart:

____

____

____

Gratitude

God Winks:

Prayer Requests:

* ________________________

* ________________________

* ________________________

Date _______________________

People on My Heart:

____
____
____

Gratitude

God Winks:

Prayer Requests:

* _______________________
* _______________________
* _______________________

Date ______________________________

People on My Heart:

____

____

____

Gratitude

God Winks:

Prayer Requests:

* ____________________________________ ◊

* ____________________________________ ◊

* ____________________________________ ◊

Date ______________________________

People on My Heart:

____

____

____

Gratitude

God Winks:

Prayer Requests:

* ______________________________ ◇

* ______________________________ ◇

* ______________________________ ◇

Date _______________________

People on My Heart:

Gratitude

God Winks:

Prayer Requests:

Date _______________________

People on My Heart:

Gratitude

God Winks:

Prayer Requests:

* _______________________
* _______________________
* _______________________

Date _______________________________

People on My Heart:

____

____

____

Gratitude

God Winks:

Prayer Requests:

* _______________________ ◇

* _______________________ ◇

* _______________________ ◇

Date ___________________________

People on My Heart:

____
____
____

Gratitude

God Winks:

Prayer Requests:

* ___________________________ ◊
  ____

* ___________________________ ◊
  ____

* ___________________________ ◊
  ____

Date ______________________________

People on My Heart:

____

____

____

Gratitude

God Winks:

Prayer Requests:

* ______________________________

* ______________________________

* ______________________________

Date ________________________________

People on My Heart:

____

____

____

Gratitude

God Winks:

Prayer Requests:

* ________________________________

* ________________________________

* ________________________________

Date _______________________

People on My Heart:

Gratitude

God Winks:

Prayer Requests:

Date ________________________________

People on My Heart:

____

____

____

Gratitude

God Winks:

Prayer Requests:

* ________________________________

* ________________________________

* ________________________________

Date ___________________________

People on My Heart:

____
____
____

Gratitude

God Winks:

Prayer Requests:

* ___________________________ ◊
____

* ___________________________ ◊
____

* ___________________________ ◊
____

Date ______________________________

People on My Heart:

Gratitude

God Winks:

Prayer Requests:

Date _______________________

People on My Heart:

____
____
____

Gratitude

God Winks:

Prayer Requests:

* _______________________ ◇
____

* _______________________ ◇
____

* _______________________ ◇
____

Date _______________________________

People on My Heart:
____
____
____

Gratitude

God Winks:

Prayer Requests:

* _______________________________ ◊
____

* _______________________________ ◊
____

* _______________________________ ◊
____

Date ________________________

People on My Heart:

____

____

____

Gratitude

God Winks:

Prayer Requests:

* ____________________ ◇

* ____________________ ◇

* ____________________ ◇

Date _______________________________

People on My Heart:

____
____
____

Gratitude

God Winks:

Prayer Requests:

* _______________________________
  ____

* _______________________________
  ____

* _______________________________
  ____

Date ___________________________

People on My Heart:

____
____
____

Gratitude

God Winks:

Prayer Requests:

* ___________________________
* ___________________________
* ___________________________

Date ___________________________

People on My Heart:

____

____

____

Gratitude

God Winks:

Prayer Requests:

* ___________________________ ◊

* ___________________________ ◊

* ___________________________ ◊

Date ______________________________

People on My Heart:

____

____

____

Gratitude

God Winks:

Prayer Requests:

* ______________________________

* ______________________________

* ______________________________

Date ________________________

People on My Heart:

____
____
____

Gratitude

God Winks:

Prayer Requests:

* ____________________
____

* ____________________
____

* ____________________
____

Date _______________________________

People on My Heart:

Gratitude

God Winks:

Prayer Requests:

*

*

*

Date ________________________________

People on My Heart:

____

____

____

Gratitude

God Winks:

Prayer Requests:

* ________________________________ ◊

* ________________________________ ◊

* ________________________________ ◊

Date _______________________

People on My Heart:

____
____
____

Gratitude

God Winks:

Prayer Requests:

* _______________________
* _______________________
* _______________________

Date _______________________

People on My Heart:

____

____

____

Gratitude

God Winks:

Prayer Requests:

* ___________________
____

* ___________________
____

* ___________________
____

Date ________________________________

People on My Heart:

Gratitude

God Winks:

Prayer Requests:

* ____________________________
* ____________________________
* ____________________________

Date _______________________________

People on My Heart:

____

____

____

Gratitude

God Winks:

Prayer Requests:

* _______________________________ ◊

* _______________________________ ◊

* _______________________________ ◊

Date _______________________________

People on My Heart:

____

____

____

Gratitude

God Winks:

Prayer Requests:

* _______________________________ ◊

* _______________________________ ◊

* _______________________________ ◊

Date ________________________

People on My Heart:

Gratitude

God Winks:

Prayer Requests:

Date ________________________

People on My Heart:

____
____
____

Gratitude

God Winks:

Prayer Requests:

* ________________________ ◊
* ________________________ ◊
* ________________________ ◊

Date _______________________________

People on My Heart:

____

____

____

Gratitude

God Winks:

Prayer Requests:

* _______________________________

* _______________________________

* _______________________________

Date ______________________________

People on My Heart:

____

____

____

Gratitude

God Winks:

Prayer Requests:

* ______________________________ ◊

* ______________________________ ◊

* ______________________________ ◊

Date ____________________________

People on My Heart:

____

____

____

Gratitude

God Winks:

Prayer Requests:

* ____________________
____

* ____________________
____

* ____________________
____

Date ___________________________

People on My Heart:

____
____
____

Gratitude

God Winks:

Prayer Requests:

* ___________________ ◊
* ___________________ ◊
* ___________________ ◊

Date ___________________________

People on My Heart:

____

____

____

Gratitude

God Winks:

Prayer Requests:

* _______________________ ◇

* _______________________ ◇

* _______________________ ◇

Date _______________________________

People on My Heart:

____

____

____

Gratitude

God Winks:

Prayer Requests:

* _______________________________ ◊

* _______________________________ ◊

* _______________________________ ◊

Date ______________________________

People on My Heart:

____
____
____

Gratitude

God Winks:

Prayer Requests:

* ______________________
____

* ______________________
____

* ______________________
____

Date _______________________________

People on My Heart:

____

____

____

Gratitude

God Winks:

Prayer Requests:

* _______________________________ ◇

* _______________________________ ◇

* _______________________________ ◇

Date ______________________________

People on My Heart:

____

____

____

Gratitude

God Winks:

Prayer Requests:

* ______________________________

* ______________________________

* ______________________________

Date _______________________________

People on My Heart:

____

____

____

Gratitude

God Winks:

Prayer Requests:

* _______________________________ ◊

* _______________________________ ◊

* _______________________________ ◊

Date _______________________________

People on My Heart:

____

____

____

Gratitude

God Winks:

Prayer Requests:

* _______________________ ◇

* _______________________ ◇

* _______________________ ◇

Date ______________________________

People on My Heart:

____

____

____

Gratitude

God Winks:

Prayer Requests:

* ______________________________ ◊

* ______________________________ ◊

* ______________________________ ◊

Date _______________________________

People on My Heart:

____

____

____

Gratitude

God Winks:

Prayer Requests:

* _______________________________ ◇

* _______________________________ ◇

* _______________________________ ◇

Date _______________________________

People on My Heart:

Gratitude

God Winks:

Prayer Requests:

*

*

*

Date ___________________________

People on My Heart:

____

____

____

Gratitude

God Winks:

Prayer Requests:

* ___________________________

* ___________________________

* ___________________________

Date ________________________

People on My Heart:

____
____
____

Gratitude

God Winks:

Prayer Requests:

* ________________________
* ________________________
* ________________________

Date _______________________________

People on My Heart:

____

____

____

Gratitude

God Winks:

Prayer Requests:

* _______________________________

* _______________________________

* _______________________________

Date _______________________________

People on My Heart:

____

____

____

Gratitude

God Winks:

Prayer Requests:

* _______________________________

* _______________________________

* _______________________________

Date _______________________________

People on My Heart:

____
____
____

Gratitude

God Winks:

Prayer Requests:

* _______________________________
* _______________________________
* _______________________________

Date ___________________________

People on My Heart:

____
____
____

Gratitude

God Winks:

Prayer Requests:

* ___________________________ ◊
* ___________________________ ◊
* ___________________________ ◊

Date _______________________________

People on My Heart:

Gratitude

God Winks:

Prayer Requests:

*

*

*

Date _______________________________

People on My Heart:

____

____

____

Gratitude

God Winks:

Prayer Requests:

* _______________________ ◊

* _______________________ ◊

* _______________________ ◊

Date ___________________________

People on My Heart:

____

____

____

Gratitude

God Winks:

Prayer Requests:

* ___________________________

* ___________________________

* ___________________________

Date ________________________

People on My Heart:

____

____

____

Gratitude

God Winks:

Prayer Requests:

* ________________________

* ________________________

* ________________________

Date ________________________________

People on My Heart:

____

____

____

Gratitude

God Winks:

Prayer Requests:

* ________________________________

* ________________________________

* ________________________________

Date _______________________________

People on My Heart:

____

____

____

Gratitude

God Winks:

Prayer Requests:

* _______________________________ ◊

* _______________________________ ◊

* _______________________________ ◊

Date _______________________________

People on My Heart:

Gratitude

God Winks:

Prayer Requests:

Date ___________________________

People on My Heart:

____
____
____

Gratitude

God Winks:

Prayer Requests:

* ___________________________ ◊
* ___________________________ ◊
* ___________________________ ◊

Date _______________________________

People on My Heart:

Gratitude

God Winks:

Prayer Requests:

* _______________________________
* _______________________________
* _______________________________

Date ___________________________

People on My Heart:

____
____
____

Gratitude

God Winks:

Prayer Requests:

* ___________________________ ◇

* ___________________________ ◇

* ___________________________ ◇

Date _______________________

People on My Heart:

____
____
____

Gratitude

God Winks:

Prayer Requests:

* _______________________
* _______________________
* _______________________

Date ___________________________

People on My Heart:

Gratitude

God Winks:

Prayer Requests:

*
*
*

Date _______________________________

People on My Heart:

____

____

____

Gratitude

God Winks:

Prayer Requests:

* _______________________________ ◊

* _______________________________ ◊

* _______________________________ ◊

Date ________________________

People on My Heart:

____

____

____

Gratitude

God Winks:

Prayer Requests:

* ________________________

* ________________________

* ________________________

Date _______________________________

People on My Heart:

____

____

____

Gratitude

God Winks:

Prayer Requests:

* _______________________

* _______________________

* _______________________

Date ________________________________

People on My Heart:

____
____
____

Gratitude

God Winks:

Prayer Requests:

* ________________________________
____

* ________________________________
____

* ________________________________
____

Date _______________________________

People on My Heart:

____

____

____

Gratitude

God Winks:

Prayer Requests:

* _______________________________ ◊

* _______________________________ ◊

* _______________________________ ◊

Date ___________________________

People on My Heart:

____
____
____

Gratitude

God Winks:

Prayer Requests:

* ___________________________
____

* ___________________________
____

* ___________________________

Date _______________________________

People on My Heart:

____

____

____

Gratitude

God Winks:

Prayer Requests:

* _______________________

* _______________________

* _______________________

Date ___________________________

People on My Heart:

____

____

____

Gratitude

God Winks:

Prayer Requests:

* ___________________________

* ___________________________

* ___________________________

Date ___________________________

People on My Heart:

____

____

____

Gratitude

God Winks:

Prayer Requests:

* _______________________ ◊

* _______________________ ◊

* _______________________ ◊

Date _______________________

People on My Heart:

Gratitude

God Winks:

Prayer Requests:

* _______________________

* _______________________

* _______________________

Date ________________________

People on My Heart:

____
____
____

Gratitude

God Winks:

Prayer Requests:

* ______________________ ◊
* ______________________ ◊
* ______________________ ◊

Date _______________________________

People on My Heart:

____

____

____

Gratitude

God Winks:

Prayer Requests:

* _______________________________________

* _______________________________________

* _______________________________________

Date ________________________________

People on My Heart:

____
____
____

Gratitude

God Winks:

Prayer Requests:

* ________________________
* ________________________
* ________________________

Date ___________________________

People on My Heart:

____

____

____

Gratitude

God Winks:

Prayer Requests:

* ___________________ ◇

* ___________________ ◇

* ___________________ ◇

Date _______________________________

People on My Heart:

____

____

____

Gratitude

God Winks:

Prayer Requests:

*_______________________ ◇

*_______________________ ◇

*_______________________ ◇

Date ___________________________

People on My Heart:

____

____

____

Gratitude

God Winks:

Prayer Requests:

* ___________________

* ___________________

* ___________________

Date ___________________________

People on My Heart:

____

____

____

Gratitude

God Winks:

Prayer Requests:

* ___________________________ ◊

* ___________________________ ◊

* ___________________________ ◊

Date ______________________________

People on My Heart:

Gratitude

God Winks:

Prayer Requests:

* ______________________________
* ______________________________
* ______________________________

Date ______________________________

People on My Heart:

____
____
____

Gratitude

God Winks:

Prayer Requests:

* ______________________________ ◊
* ______________________________ ◊
* ______________________________ ◊

Date ___________________________

People on My Heart:

____

____

____

Gratitude

God Winks:

Prayer Requests:

* ___________________ ◊

* ___________________ ◊

* ___________________ ◊

Date ___________________________

People on My Heart:

____
____
____

Gratitude

God Winks:

Prayer Requests:

* ______________________________
* ______________________________
* ______________________________

Date ______________________________

People on My Heart:

____
____
____

Gratitude

God Winks:

Prayer Requests:

* ______________________
* ______________________
* ______________________

Date _______________________________

People on My Heart:

____

____

____

Gratitude

God Winks:

Prayer Requests:

* _______________________ ◊

* _______________________ ◊

* _______________________ ◊

Date ___________________________

People on My Heart:

____

____

____

Gratitude

God Winks:

Prayer Requests:

* ___________________________

* ___________________________

* ___________________________

Date ____________________________

People on My Heart:

____

____

____

Gratitude

God Winks:

Prayer Requests:

* ____________________

* ____________________

* ____________________

Date _______________________

People on My Heart:

Gratitude

God Winks:

Prayer Requests:

Date ________________________________

People on My Heart:

Gratitude

God Winks:

Prayer Requests:

Date _______________________

People on My Heart:

Gratitude

God Winks:

Prayer Requests:

Date _______________________

People on My Heart:

Gratitude

God Winks:

Prayer Requests:

* _______________________
* _______________________
* _______________________

Date ___________________________

People on My Heart:

____

____

____

Gratitude

God Winks:

Prayer Requests:

* ________________________________ ◇

* ________________________________ ◇

* ________________________________ ◇

Date ______________________________

People on My Heart:

____

____

____

Gratitude

God Winks:

Prayer Requests:

* ______________________________

* ______________________________

* ______________________________

Date _______________________________

People on My Heart:

____

____

____

Gratitude

God Winks:

Prayer Requests:

* _______________________________ ◇

* _______________________________ ◇

* _______________________________ ◇

Date ________________________________

People on My Heart:

____

____

____

Gratitude

God Winks:

Prayer Requests:

* _______________________

* _______________________

* _______________________

Date ________________________

People on My Heart:

Gratitude

God Winks:

Prayer Requests:

* ________________________

* ________________________

* ________________________

Date _______________________________

People on My Heart:

____

____

____

Gratitude

God Winks:

Prayer Requests:

* _______________________ ◇

* _______________________ ◇

* _______________________ ◇

Date ___________________________

People on My Heart:

____

____

____

Gratitude

God Winks:

Prayer Requests:

* ___________________________

* ___________________________

* ___________________________

Date ___________________________

People on My Heart:

____

____

____

Gratitude

God Winks:

Prayer Requests:

* ___________________________

* ___________________________

* ___________________________

Date ___________________________

People on My Heart:

____

____

____

Gratitude

God Winks:

Prayer Requests:

* ___________________________

* ___________________________

* ___________________________

Date ________________________

People on My Heart:

____

____

____

Gratitude

God Winks:

Prayer Requests:

* ________________________

* ________________________

* ________________________

Date _______________________________

People on My Heart:

____
____
____

Gratitude

God Winks:

Prayer Requests:

* _______________________
* _______________________
* _______________________

Date _______________________

People on My Heart:

____
____
____

Gratitude

God Winks:

Prayer Requests:

* _______________________
____

* _______________________
____

* _______________________
____

Date ___________________________

People on My Heart:

____
____
____

Gratitude

God Winks:

Prayer Requests:

* ___________________________
* ___________________________
* ___________________________

Date ________________________________

People on My Heart:

____

____

____

Gratitude

God Winks:

Prayer Requests:

* ________________________

* ________________________

* ________________________

Date _______________________

People on My Heart:

Gratitude

God Winks:

Prayer Requests:

*
*
*

Date _______________________________

People on My Heart:

____

____

____

Gratitude

God Winks:

Prayer Requests:

* _______________________________

* _______________________________

* _______________________________

Date _______________________________

People on My Heart:

____

____

____

Gratitude

God Winks:

Prayer Requests:

* _______________________________

* _______________________________

* _______________________________

Date ______________________________

People on My Heart:

____

____

____

Gratitude

God Winks:

Prayer Requests:

* ______________________

* ______________________

* ______________________

Date _______________________________

People on My Heart:

____

____

____

Gratitude

God Winks:

Prayer Requests:

* _______________________________

* _______________________________

* _______________________________

Date _______________________________

People on My Heart:

____

____

____

Gratitude

God Winks:

Prayer Requests:

* _______________________________

* _______________________________

* _______________________________

Date ______________________________

People on My Heart:

____
____
____

Gratitude

God Winks:

Prayer Requests:

* ______________________________
* ______________________________
* ______________________________

Date _______________________________

People on My Heart:

Gratitude

God Winks:

Prayer Requests:

*

Date ______________________________

People on My Heart:

____

____

____

Gratitude

God Winks:

Prayer Requests:

* ________________________ ◇

* ________________________ ◇

* ________________________ ◇

Date ___________________________

People on My Heart:

____

____

____

Gratitude

God Winks:

Prayer Requests:

* ___________________________ ◊

* ___________________________ ◊

* ___________________________ ◊

Date _______________________

People on My Heart:

____

____

____

Gratitude

God Winks:

Prayer Requests:

* _______________________

* _______________________

* _______________________

Date ___________________________

People on My Heart:

____
____
____

Gratitude

God Winks:

Prayer Requests:

* ___________________________ ◊
* ___________________________ ◊
* ___________________________ ◊

Date ______________________________

People on My Heart:

Gratitude

God Winks:

Prayer Requests:

* ______________________________
* ______________________________
* ______________________________

Date ________________________

People on My Heart:

Gratitude

God Winks:

Prayer Requests:

*

*

*

Date ___________________________

People on My Heart:

____
____
____

Gratitude

God Winks:

Prayer Requests:

* _______________________ ◊
* _______________________ ◊
* _______________________ ◊

Date _______________________________

People on My Heart:

____
____
____

Gratitude

God Winks:

Prayer Requests:

* _______________________
____

* _______________________
____

* _______________________
____

Date ______________________________

People on My Heart:

____

____

____

Gratitude

God Winks:

Prayer Requests:

* ______________________________ ◊

* ______________________________ ◊

* ______________________________ ◊

Date ___________________________

People on My Heart:

____

____

____

Gratitude

God Winks:

Prayer Requests:

* ___________________________

* ___________________________

* ___________________________

Date ___________________________

People on My Heart:

____

____

____

Gratitude

God Winks:

Prayer Requests:

* ___________________ ◇

* ___________________ ◇

* ___________________ ◇

Date ________________________________

People on My Heart:

____

____

____

Gratitude

God Winks:

Prayer Requests:

* ________________________ ◊

* ________________________ ◊

* ________________________ ◊

Date _______________________________

People on My Heart:

____

____

____

Gratitude

God Winks:

Prayer Requests:

* _______________________________

* _______________________________

* _______________________________

Date _______________________

People on My Heart:

____

____

____

Gratitude

God Winks:

Prayer Requests:

* _______________________

* _______________________

* _______________________

Date _______________________

People on My Heart:

Gratitude

God Winks:

Prayer Requests:

*

*

*

Date ___________________________

People on My Heart:

____
____
____

Gratitude

God Winks:

Prayer Requests:

* ______________________
____

* ______________________
____

* ______________________
____

Date ___________________________

People on My Heart:

____

____

____

Gratitude

God Winks:

Prayer Requests:

* _______________ ◊

* _______________ ◊

* _______________ ◊

Date ___________________________

People on My Heart:

____
____
____

Gratitude

God Winks:

Prayer Requests:

* _______________________

* _______________________

* _______________________

Date _______________________________

People on My Heart:

____

____

____

Gratitude

God Winks:

Prayer Requests:

* _______________________ ◊

* _______________________ ◊

* _______________________ ◊

Date ___________________________

People on My Heart:

____

____

____

Gratitude

God Winks:

Prayer Requests:

* ___________________

* ___________________

* ___________________

Date _______________________________

People on My Heart:

Gratitude

God Winks:

Prayer Requests:

* _______________________________
* _______________________________
* _______________________________

Date ___________________________

People on My Heart:

____

____

____

Gratitude

God Winks:

Prayer Requests:

* ___________________________
____

* ___________________________
____

* ___________________________
____

Date ________________________________

People on My Heart:

____

____

____

Gratitude

God Winks:

Prayer Requests:

* ____________________________ ◇

* ____________________________ ◇

* ____________________________ ◇

Date _______________________________

People on My Heart:

____

____

____

Gratitude

God Winks:

Prayer Requests:

*_______________________

*_______________________

*_______________________

Date ___________________________

People on My Heart:

____
____
____

Gratitude

God Winks:

Prayer Requests:

* ___________________________ ◊
* ___________________________ ◊
* ___________________________ ◊

Date ___________________________

People on My Heart:

____

____

____

Gratitude

God Winks:

Prayer Requests:

* ___________________________

* ___________________________

* ___________________________

Date ______________________________

People on My Heart:

Gratitude

God Winks:

Prayer Requests:

* ______________________________
* ______________________________
* ______________________________

Date _______________________

People on My Heart:

Gratitude

God Winks:

Prayer Requests:

Date _______________________

People on My Heart:

Gratitude

God Winks:

Prayer Requests:

Date _______________________________

People on My Heart:
____
____
____

Gratitude

God Winks:

Prayer Requests:
* _______________________________
* _______________________________
* _______________________________

Date ________________________

People on My Heart:

____
____
____

Gratitude

God Winks:

Prayer Requests:

* ________________________

* ________________________

* ________________________

Date ________________________

People on My Heart:

____

____

____

Gratitude

God Winks:

Prayer Requests:

* ________________________

* ________________________

* ________________________

Date ______________________________

People on My Heart:

____

____

____

Gratitude

God Winks:

Prayer Requests:

* ______________________________
____

* ______________________________
____

* ______________________________
____

Date ___________________________

People on My Heart:

____
____
____

Gratitude

God Winks:

Prayer Requests:

* ___________________________
  ____

* ___________________________
  ____

* ___________________________
  ____

Date ________________________________

People on My Heart:

Gratitude

God Winks:

Prayer Requests:

*

*

*

Date _______________________________

People on My Heart:

____
____
____

Gratitude

God Winks:

Prayer Requests:

* _______________________________ ◊
* _______________________________ ◊
* _______________________________ ◊

Date ________________________

People on My Heart:

Gratitude

God Winks:

Prayer Requests:

* ________________________
* ________________________
* ________________________

Date ___________________________

People on My Heart:

____

____

____

Gratitude

God Winks:

Prayer Requests:

* ______________________

* ______________________

* ______________________

Date _______________________

People on My Heart:

Gratitude

God Winks:

Prayer Requests:

* _______________________
* _______________________
* _______________________

Date ___________________________

People on My Heart:
____
____
____

Gratitude

God Winks:

Prayer Requests:
* ______________________ ◊
* ______________________ ◊
* ______________________ ◊

Date ______________________________

People on My Heart:

____

____

____

Gratitude

God Winks:

Prayer Requests:

*

*

*

Date _______________________

People on My Heart:

Gratitude

God Winks:

Prayer Requests:

*

*

*

Date ___________________________

People on My Heart:

____

____

____

Gratitude

God Winks:

Prayer Requests:

* ___________________________
____

* ___________________________
____

* ___________________________
____

Date ________________________________

People on My Heart:

____

____

____

Gratitude

God Winks:

Prayer Requests:

* ________________________

* ________________________

* ________________________

Date _______________________

People on My Heart:

Gratitude

God Winks:

Prayer Requests:

Date _______________________

People on My Heart:

____

____

____

Gratitude

God Winks:

Prayer Requests:

* _______________________

* _______________________

* _______________________

Date _______________________

People on My Heart:

Gratitude

God Winks:

Prayer Requests:

* _______________________ ◊

* _______________________ ◊

* _______________________ ◊

Date ___________________________

People on My Heart:

____
____
____

Gratitude

God Winks:

Prayer Requests:

* ___________________________ ◊
* ___________________________ ◊
* ___________________________ ◊

Date _______________________

People on My Heart:

Gratitude

God Winks:

Prayer Requests:

* _______________________
* _______________________
* _______________________